AF228188

GROWING GARDENS

Herb Gardens

BY SAMANTHA S. BELL

Kids Core
An Imprint of Abdo Publishing
abdobooks.com

abdobooks.com

Printed in the United States of America, North Mankato, Minnesota.
052025
092025

Cover Photo: Shutterstock Images
Interior Photos: Shutterstock Images, 4–5, 7, 10–11, 18, 21, 22–23, 24, 28 (top), 28 (bottom), 29 (top), 29 (bottom); Viktoriia Hnatiuk/iStockphoto, 8; Joanna Tkaczuk/Shutterstock Images, 12; Anna Stills/iStockphoto, 15; Rich Legg/iStockphoto, 16; iStockphoto, 19, 20, 26 (basil, cilantro, mint), 26 (mustard)

Editor: Christa Kelly
Series Designer: Katharine Hale

Library of Congress Control Number: 2024948999

Publisher's Cataloging-in-Publication Data

Names: Bell, Samantha S., author.
Title: Herb gardens / by Samantha S. Bell
Description: Minneapolis, Minnesota: Abdo Publishing, 2026 | Series: Growing gardens | Includes online resources and index.
Identifiers: ISBN 9781098297404 (lib. bdg.) | ISBN 9798384919926 (ebook)
Subjects: LCSH: Gardens--Juvenile literature. | Gardening--Juvenile literature. | Herbs--Juvenile literature. | Horticulture--Juvenile literature.
Classification: DDC 635.7--dc23

CONTENTS

Most herbs are easy to grow.
This makes them great for
beginner gardeners.

CHAPTER 1

Growing Fresh Flavors

Jack enjoyed cooking with his mom. They used herbs to give their dishes lots of flavor. Usually, they would buy dried herbs from the store. But Jack's mom said they could start an herb garden! With a garden, Jack would have fresh herbs to use.

Jack went to the backyard. He looked around for the best place to put the garden. He thought about growing the herbs near the kitchen door. That way, they would be close by when he wanted them. But his backyard had a lot of trees. It was shady most of the day.

Jack noticed how sunny it was in front of his house. He decided to plant his garden in a container near the front steps. Jack's mom gave him two medium pots with holes in the bottoms.

Herb or Spice?

Though herbs and spices are both used in cooking, they are not the same. Herbs come from the leaves of plants. Spices come from the roots, flowers, fruits, seeds, and bark. Spices usually have stronger flavors than herbs.

First, Jack filled the containers with soil. Then he and his mom went to the store to buy seeds. Jack picked basil and cilantro. He planted the seeds in the pots. He could not wait to start using his fresh herbs!

The Many Uses of Herbs

Herbs are plants that add flavor to food or create pleasant smells. Some people use herbs when they cook to season their food.

Herbs are also used to make teas. They can even be used in perfumes and medicine.

Growing herbs teaches people about gardening. It also gives people access to fresh food. Growing herbs is a fun activity for kids and their families.

Lara Hermanson co-owns a gardening company in California. She says:

> Herb gardens are wonderful ways for beginning gardeners to develop their skills, as they are less intense and detailed to maintain than, say, a vegetable or cut flower garden.

Source: Perri Ormont Blumberg. "17 Herb Garden Ideas to Make Your Secret Cottage Dreams Come True." *Architectural Digest*, 22 Apr. 2024, architecturaldigest.com. Accessed 17 Oct. 2024.

Comparing Texts

Does this quote support the information in this chapter? Or does it give a different perspective? Explain your answer in two to three sentences.

Many gardeners make maps
showing where each plant
will go. This helps people plan
their gardens.

CHAPTER 2

Planning an Herb Garden

The first step in planning an herb garden is deciding where to grow the plants. Some people grow herbs in their yards. Others grow herbs on patios or in window boxes. Some people even grow herbs indoors!

Plants use sunlight to make energy in a process called photosynthesis. They use the energy to grow.

When deciding where to grow herbs, people should think about how much sunlight different areas receive. Most herbs grow best in sunny locations. They need at least six hours of sunlight each day. More sunlight is even better.

Sunlight helps herbs develop oils. The oils make the herbs' **fragrances** and flavors stronger.

People growing plants inside can place herbs next to a sunny window. Gardeners growing plants outside should pay attention to any obstacles that might block sunlight. Houses, fences, and trees may block some light. But they can also protect the plants from the wind. Strong winds can damage herbs.

Growing Herbs Indoors

Herbs can grow indoors all year long. They can be placed near a window for six hours of sunlight. They can also grow with 12 to 16 hours of **artificial** light.

Next, gardeners should decide how to grow their plants. Some people grow herbs directly in the ground. Others grow herbs in containers. Herbs can be grown in almost any type of container. But the best containers have holes in the bottom to let extra water drain out. These holes give the plant drainage. This means any extra water can leave the soil.

If a container does not have drainage, extra water may harm the plant's roots. The water can stop the plant from taking in air or **nutrients**. This causes the roots to rot. The plant may die.

Types of Herbs

Once people have chosen a location for their garden, they can choose which herbs to plant.

Some herb plants are small. Others can grow to be the size
of bushes.

Gardeners should grow herbs they enjoy eating.

Herbs generally fall into three main categories. Gardeners can choose annual, biennial, or perennial herbs.

An annual is a plant that goes through its **life cycle** in one growing season. It needs to be replanted each year. Some examples of annuals are basil, dill, and cilantro.

A biennial is a plant that goes through its life cycle in two growing seasons. It grows leaves in the first season. It grows flowers in the second season. Biennial herbs include parsley and evening primrose.

Some herbs grow for many years. They are called perennials. Perennials include mint, thyme, rosemary, and oregano. In warmer **climates**, perennials may stay green all year.

In colder climates, they may behave more like annuals and die in the winter. However, some will sprout again in the spring.

Herbs are also grouped into plant families. Plants in the same families grow well together. They are often planted near each other.

Many herbs used in cooking are members of the mint, carrot, and mustard families. Herbs in the mint family include mint, basil, rosemary, and lavender. These plants are bushy.

Some gardeners bring their plants inside when the weather gets cold. This is called overwintering.

Mint leaves can be used to make desserts such as homemade ice cream.

Many have fragrant leaves. Most of them can grow in dry soil and heat. Herbs in the carrot family include dill, parsley, cilantro, and fennel. These plants tend to grow tall and thin. They need deep and wet soil. Herbs in the mustard

family include horseradish and mustard. They grow best in cool climates. Their leaves smell like mustard.

Further Evidence

Look at the website below. Does it give any new evidence to support Chapter Two?

Growing Herbs

abdocorelibrary.com/herb-gardens

Herbs that grow in cool climates can be planted outside in early spring. Herbs that grow in warm climates can be planted outdoors in late spring.

CHAPTER 3

Growing Herbs

Once the garden has been planned, it's time to start planting! There are several ways to start growing herbs. Some people grow herbs from seeds. Seeds can be bought from stores or collected from plants. Annuals are often started from seeds.

Herbs can also be planted as young plants, or seedlings. When planting seedlings, people should place them deep enough to cover the top of the roots with soil. The seedlings should have space between them to grow. Herbs can also be started from pieces of stems called stem cuttings.

After herbs are planted, they need to be watered regularly. Gardeners should be careful to water the dirt around the plant, not the plant's leaves. This way, water can go to the roots. The roots then supply water to the rest of the plant. If an herb does not have enough water, it will **wilt**. Herbs grown outdoors in pots may need more water than herbs grown in the ground. This is because pots cannot hold as much water as the ground can.

Stem Cuttings

To grow herbs from stem cuttings, gardeners first cut a stem about three to four inches (8–10 cm) long. Then the lower part of the stem is dipped into a special substance that helps roots grow. The stem is planted in damp soil in a warm location.

How to Harvest

	Herb	Part to Take	Tool
	Basil	Stem with leaves	Fingers or clippers
	Cilantro	Mature stem or individual leaves	Fingers or clippers
	Mint	Top four to eight inches (10–20 cm) of a stem	Clippers
	Mustard	Leaves or seed pods	Clippers

Different herbs should be harvested in different ways.

Harvesting Herbs

When the herbs are fully grown, they can be harvested. Harvesting is the process of gathering herbs to use. Herbs used for cooking can be taken from the plant throughout the growing season. This also helps keep the plants healthy.

Herb gardens provide fresh food and an opportunity to work with plants. With proper care, an herb garden can grow almost anywhere. Whether planted in the ground or in containers, herb gardening can be enjoyed by people of all ages.

Explore Online

Visit the website below. Does it give any new information about harvesting herbs that wasn't in Chapter Three?

Harvesting Herbs

abdocorelibrary.com/herb-gardens

Garden Plants

Rosemary

Rosemary is a perennial herb. It is part of the mint family. It is used in foods, medicines, and perfumes.

Horseradish

Horseradish is a perennial herb. It is part of the mustard family. It is used in foods and medicines.

Cilantro

Cilantro is an annual herb. It is part of the carrot family. It is used to flavor soups and meat dishes.

English lavender

English lavender is a perennial herb. It is part of the mint family. It is used in soaps, perfumes, and drinks.

Glossary

artificial
made by humans

climates
areas with specific weather patterns

fragrances
scents

life cycle
the stages a plant goes through from the time it first starts growing until it dies

nutrients
substances that living things need to grow and stay healthy

wilt
in plants, to droop or bend, often when the plant is unhealthy

Online Resources

To learn more about growing herb gardens, visit our free resource websites below.

Visit **abdocorelibrary.com** or scan this QR code for free Common Core resources for teachers and students, including vetted activities, multimedia, and booklinks, for deeper subject comprehension.

Visit **abdobooklinks.com** or scan this QR code for free additional online weblinks for further learning. These links are routinely monitored and updated to provide the most current information available.

Learn More

Brown, Molly Meehan. *Herbal Activities for Kids: 50 Nature Crafts, Recipes, and Garden Projects.* Storey, 2024.

Gadzekpo, Darryl and Ella Phillips. *From Plant to Plate.* DK, 2024.

Index

About the Author

Samantha S. Bell lives in the foothills of the Blue Ridge Mountains with her family and four cats. She has written more than 150 nonfiction books for students in kindergarten through high school. She loves growing herbs on her patio.